MICHAEL JACKSON INSPIRING BIOGRAPHY FOR KIDS

The King Of Pop's Journey From a Small Town to Global Fame - Incredible Story Of Talent, Hardwork and Giving Back

Corey Ashford

Copyright © 2025 Corey Ashford. All Rights Reserved
No part of this publication may be reproduced, or transmitted in any
form or by any means, including photocopying, recording, or other
electronic or mechanical methods, without the prior written
permission of the publisher

CW01501761

Disclaimer:

This book is an unofficial biography of Michael Jackson and is intended for informational and educational purposes only. It is not affiliated with, authorized, or endorsed by Michael Jackson's estate, family, or any official representatives. All information included is based on publicly available sources, historical records, and well-documented events from Michael Jackson's life.

While every effort has been made to ensure accuracy, this book does not claim to provide a definitive account of Michael Jackson's life and career. Any interpretations or reflections are meant to inspire readers and encourage learning from his journey. The book is written for young readers to celebrate Michael Jackson's impact on music, dance, and philanthropy while promoting positive life lessons.

Table Of Contents

Introduction   6

Chapter 1   8
A Star is Born

Chapter 2   12
The Jackson 5 Journey

Chapter 3   18
Stepping Into the Spotlight

Chapter 4   24
Thriller - The Record Breaking Album

Chapter 5   30
The Power Of Dance and Music

Chapter 6   36
Spreading Love and Helping Others

Chapter 7   42
The Neverland Dream

Chapter 8   48
Overcoming Challenges

Chapter 9   54
The Legacy Lives On

Chapter 10   60
Fun Extras & Self Reflective Prompts

Introduction

Have you ever heard a song so amazing that it makes you want to dance, sing, and dream big all at the same time? That's the magic of Michael Jackson—a boy from a small town who became the most famous entertainer in the world! Michael wasn't just a singer or a dancer—he was a legend. He created songs that touched hearts, invented dance moves no one had ever seen before, and used his success to help people in need. From his early days as a superstar kid in The Jackson 5 to becoming the King of Pop, Michael's journey is a story of talent, hard work, kindness, and never giving up.

This book is packed with exciting stories about Michael's life, including how he started singing at just five years old and became a superstar as a child, how he created record-breaking music like Thriller—the best-selling album in history, and how he changed the world of dance with unforgettable moves like the Moonwalk. You'll also discover how he used his fame to help children, protect animals, and make the world a better place.

But this book isn't just about learning Michael's story—it's about learning about how his journey teaches us powerful life lessons, such as dreaming big and believing in yourself, working hard to make your dreams come true, being kind and helping those in need, and never giving up, even when things get tough. To help you apply these lessons to your own life, this book includes special self-reflection prompts that will encourage you to think about what you've learned and how you can use Michael's story to inspire your own journey.

If you love music, dancing, and stories about people who changed the world, this book is for YOU! Get ready to dive into the incredible life of Michael Jackson and discover how his music, moves, and message continue to inspire millions —even today. So turn the page, start reading, and feel the magic of Michael Jackson!

Chapter 1

A Star Is Born

A little boy was born on August 29, 1958, in the small city of Gary, Indiana. He would change the music world forever. Michael Joseph Jackson was his name. His family had ten kids, and he was the eighth. Music was all around him from the time he was born.

Joseph Jackson (Joe) and Katherine Jackson took care of their big family with a lot of work. Joe, his dad, worked long hours at a steel mill to support his family. But he wasn't just a mill worker; he loved music very much. In the years before Michael was born, Joe played guitar in a small band called The Falcons. He wanted to be a musician one day. Katherine was his mother. She was nice and gentle, and she loved to sing and play the piano. She had a beautiful voice and often sang church songs around the house.

There wasn't a lot of money in the Jackson family, but they were close. There was always a lot of life, laughter, and music in their house. Michael and his brothers spent their days playing together, but music was always at the heart of their home.

Growing Up in Gary, Indiana

The Jackson family lived in a tiny, two-bedroom house on 2300 Jackson Street in Gary, Indiana. It was a simple home, much too small for such a big family, but it was filled with love and dreams.

Gary was an industry city, known for its steel mills. It wasn't the safest or richest place to grow up, but the Jackson children made the best of what they had. They didn't have expensive toys or big yards to play in, but they had each other.

Since money was tight, the Jackson kids had to share everything—beds, clothes, and even food. Sometimes, their father would come home tired and stressed from work, and he expected his children to be disciplined and responsible. Joe was strict, but he also had a dream: he wanted his children to become musicians and make a better life for themselves.

Despite the difficulties, Michael was a happy and playful child. He was funny, lively, and full of life. He loved to dance and sing, often putting on little shows for his family. His mother, Katherine, noticed his beautiful singing voice early on and supported him. She played records of great singers like Sam Cooke, Ray Charles, and Jackie Wilson, and little Michael would listen carefully, trying to copy their voices.

But Michael's childhood wasn't just about fun and music. He and his brothers had to work hard. Their father pushed them to practice their music every day, often making them prepare for hours after school. Michael was younger than most of his brothers, but he didn't let that stop him—he wanted to be the best.

A Family Full of Music

Music was the heart and soul of the Jackson family. Almost every member had a gift for singing or playing an instrument. Joe, recognizing this, chose to form a band with his sons. He thought that their musical talent could be their way out of poverty.

Michael's bigger brothers—Jackie, Tito, and Jermaine—started practicing music under their father's strict guidance. Joe made sure they took their rehearsals seriously, giving them discipline and stage presence. Marlon and Michael, the younger boys at the time, watched in excitement, dreaming of being a part of the group.

It didn't take long for Joe to notice something special about Michael. Even though he was small, he had an incredible voice—powerful, soulful, and full of feeling. He could sing with the depth and feeling of an adult, and he had an unmatched sense of rhythm.

Soon, Michael was added to the group, and The Jackson 5 was born. Even though he was the youngest, his energy, charisma, and singing quickly made him the star of the group.

The Jackson family spent countless nights playing in their tiny living room, turning it into a mini music studio. Their mother, Katherine, cheered them on, while their father made sure they worked hard to perfect every song and dance move. They performed at neighborhood talent shows, school events, and even small clubs. People couldn't believe how skilled they were—especially little Michael!

Though life in Gary was tough, music gave Michael and his family a sense of hope. It was the beginning of something incredible—the start of a trip that would take them from their small home in Indiana to the biggest stages in the world.

Michael was just a young boy, but his passion, dedication, and love for music would soon make him a worldwide superstar. He was a star in the making, ready to shine brighter than anyone ever dreamed.

Chapter 2

The Jackson 5 Journey

By the time Michael Jackson was just five years old, it was clear to everyone around him that he was a special child. He had a voice that was strong, soulful, and full of emotion —far beyond his years. He could hit high notes with ease, and his ability to feel the music and show emotions through his singing was something rare. His father, Joe Jackson, knew he had found something extraordinary.

Michael finally joined his older brothers Jackie, Tito, Jermaine, and Marlon in their family band, which they named The Jackson 5. At first, Michael wasn't the lead singer—his brother Jermaine held that role. But as they kept rehearsing, it became clear that Michael had something unique. He didn't just sing—he acted. His voice, energy, and charisma caught people's attention, and soon, he became the lead singer of the group.

The Jackson boys practiced for hours every day, sometimes late into the night. Joe was a strict boss, making sure every dance step was perfect and every note was sung just right. He pushed them hard, believing that their success rested on discipline and hard work. Michael, despite being the youngest, kept up with his older brothers and often outshined them with his natural ability.

Before they knew it, The Jackson 5 started performing at neighborhood talent shows, high school dances, and small clubs around their hometown of Gary, Indiana. The more they performed, the more people noticed them. They won almost every talent show they joined, with Michael's electrifying performances leaving audiences amazed.

Soon, they were invited to play in bigger cities like Chicago, St. Louis, and New York. Their reputation was rising, and they were getting closer to their big break.

The Big Break

The Jackson 5's journey to stardom took a major turn when they were found by Bobby Taylor, a singer and producer who was impressed by their talent. He introduced them to Berry Gordy, the founder of Motown Records, one of the biggest and most important record labels in the world at the time.

Motown was home to some of the best music legends, including Stevie Wonder, The Supremes, The Temptations, and Marvin Gaye. Berry Gordy saw something special in The Jackson 5—especially in Michael. He knew right away that this young boy had the ability to be a superstar.

In 1968, The Jackson 5 finally signed a record deal with Motown Records, and their lives changed forever. The family packed up and moved from their small house in Gary, Indiana, to Los Angeles, California, where they would begin recording music and training for their professional jobs.

Under Motown, the Jackson brothers got expert training in singing, dancing, and stage performance. They worked with the best producers, songwriters, and choreographers in the business. Michael, still just a child, had to learn how to be a skilled entertainer. But he wasn't just learning—he was leading. His voice, stage presence, and ability to connect with crowds made him the star of the group.

In 1969, The Jackson 5 launched their first big hit, "I Want You Back." The song became an instant hit, reaching No. 1 on the Billboard charts. The group followed up with three more hit songs: "ABC," "The Love You Save," and "I'll Be There." Each song became a No. 1 hit, making history as The Jackson 5 became the first group in music history to have their first four hits reach No. 1 on the charts.

With their catchy songs, smooth dance moves, and matching colorful outfits, The Jackson 5 became a global sensation. Kids and adults everywhere loved their music, and Michael, with his bright smile and incredible voice, became a famous kid.

Touring the World
With their music topping the charts, The Jackson 5 set off on their first big tour. They played in sold-out arenas across the United States, Europe, and even Japan. Everywhere they went, fans screamed their names, held up pictures, and tried to catch a glimpse of the young stars.

Michael, despite being the youngest member, was the most captivating artist on stage. He danced like James Brown, sang with the soul of legends, and had an energy that made the people go wild. People couldn't believe that such a small child had such a big personality.

The Jackson 5 appeared on some of the biggest television shows of the time, including The Ed Sullivan Show, where millions of people watched Michael and his brothers perform on national TV. Their fame kept rising, and they were soon traveling around the world, performing in countries like France, England, and Brazil.

Michael loved singing, but touring wasn't always easy. He had to balance school with concerts, long practices, and interviews. He often missed out on normal childhood experiences—he couldn't play outside like other kids or go to the park without being surrounded by fans.

Even though touring was exhausting, Michael lived for the show. He loved making people happy with his music, and every night, he gave his best show.

As The Jackson 5 continued their success, Michael started to stand out more and more. People weren't just fans of The Jackson 5—they were fans of Michael Jackson. He was charming, talented, and had a special link with audiences that couldn't be ignored.

By the early 1970s, Michael was already one of the most popular kids in the world. But deep down, he had even bigger dreams. He loved being part of The Jackson 5, but he knew that one day, he wanted to make his own music, his own style, and his own legacy.

Little did the world know, this young boy from Gary, Indiana, was only just starting.

Chapter 3

Stepping Into the Spotlight

Michael Jackson had already accomplished what most musicians could only hope for by the middle of the 1970s. He had topped the music charts, toured the world, and performed in front of enormous crowds as the lead singer of The Jackson 5. Deep down, though, Michael realized he could do more as an independent artist as well as a member of a group.

Michael began to feel as he got older that he wanted to experiment with his own style and find methods to express himself outside of The Jackson 5's music. He had a vision of his own, but he also loved his brothers and appreciated all that they had accomplished together. He aspired to write music that was uniquely his own, music that would transcend conventions and move listeners in a way that had never been done before.

The Jackson 5's music and image were always under the authority of Motown, the record label that had aided in their ascent to stardom. They made decisions on the brothers' attire as well as the music and performances. However, Michael felt constrained as he grew older. He desired to contribute to the creation of his own music and sound.

Michael began his solo career in 1971 with the release of his debut album, Got to Be There, while still a member of The Jackson 5. His voice and manner were already changing around the age of thirteen. Songs like "Ben" and "Rockin' Robin" demonstrated his independence. The world was starting to realize that Michael Jackson was more than simply a child celebrity; he was a budding musical genius. His brilliance was indisputable.

Michael continues to perform alongside his siblings and concentrate on solo projects over the ensuing years. However, by the late 1970s, it was obvious that he needed to take center stage on his own.

Making His Own Music

The Jackson 5 changed their name to The Jacksons and signed with Epic Records after leaving Motown Records in 1975. They had more creative flexibility as a result of this change, and Michael started to write and produce more of the group's songs. His real creative breakthrough, however, occurred when he met Quincy Jones, a great producer who would forever alter his career.

Quincy and Michael first crossed paths while working on the 1978 movie The Wiz, in which Michael costarred with Diana Ross as the Scarecrow. Respected composer and producer Quincy Jones identified Michael's undeveloped ability and his potential to become one of the greatest musicians of all time.

They started collaborating on Off the Wall (1979), Michael's debut adult solo album. His career took a significant shift with this record. It produced a novel and captivating sound by fusing pop, funk, R&B, and disco. Over 20 million copies of the album were sold worldwide, and tracks like "Don't Stop 'Til You Get Enough" and "Rock with You" became enormous hits.

Off the Wall demonstrated that Michael was a real artist with an own voice and style, not merely a former child star. A new Michael Jackson was emerging to the world—one who was fearless, creative, and willing to test limits. However, this was just the start.

Being successful was not enough for Michael; he aspired to become the greatest entertainer in history. He put spent endless hours honing his vocal skills, studying dance greats like Sammy Davis Jr., Fred Astaire, and James Brown, and pushing himself to make something that had never been seen before.

Michael had set the scene with Off the Wall. He would, however, irrevocably alter music with his subsequent record.

The Rise of the King of Pop
Michael Jackson's album "Thriller," which would go down in history, was published in 1982.

Thriller, which was once again produced by Quincy Jones, was a cultural revolution rather than merely an album. It had it all: catchy rhythms, catchy tunes, and innovative production. But Michael himself was what really made it legendary.

Each song on Thriller was thoughtfully written to highlight Michael's abilities and originality. Every song, from the dramatic and eerie "Thriller" to the thrilling "Beat It" to the sentimental and mellow "Human Nature," had something new and intriguing to offer. One of Michael's most well-known songs, "Billie Jean," which recounted the enigmatic tale of a lady who claimed he was the father of her child, was also featured on the album.

However, Michael's ability to bring the songs to life was what really made Thriller renowned, not simply the music. He brought innovative music videos to the globe, transforming them into mini-movies with previously unheard-of special effects, intricate dance routines, and cinematic storytelling.

With its terrifying zombie dance and horror-movie concept, the music video for "Thriller" quickly became a classic. While "Billie Jean" introduced the world to one of Michael's most renowned performances—the Moonwalk—"Beat It" featured his well-known dance moves.

When Michael performed "Billie Jean" on the Motown 25: Yesterday, Today, Forever television special in 1983, he revealed the Moonwalk. The world watched in awe as he glided backward across the stage with ease. His status as a musical and dance star was solidified in that one moment.

With more than 70 million copies sold globally, Thriller became the best-selling album of all time. Michael became the most well-known performer in the world after it took home a record-breaking eight Grammy Awards.

Beyond simply shattering records, Michael made a lasting impact on music. As one of the first Black musicians to have their music videos included on MTV, he broke down barriers based on race. His popularity paved the way for upcoming Black musicians.

Michael Jackson had formally established himself as the King of Pop thanks to his unparalleled skill, groundbreaking songs, and captivating dancing moves.

It was quite remarkable how Michael Jackson went from being a little boy in Gary, Indiana, to becoming the world's largest superstar. Through perseverance, hard effort, and an unwavering love of music, he revolutionized the entertainment sector and left a legacy that continues to motivate millions of people today.

But there was still more to his narrative. Michael would go on to redefine what it meant to be a worldwide celebrity with his subsequent albums, tours, and charitable endeavors.

He was a legend, a visionary, and an artist in addition to being a singer.

The world will never be the same with the rise of the King of Pop.

Chapter 4

Thriller – The Record-Breaking Album

Michael Jackson had already proven himself as an amazing talent. He had captivated audiences as a child star with The Jackson 5, and his first adult solo album, Off the Wall, had made him one of the most exciting artists of his age. But Michael wanted more—he wanted to make history.

With his next release, he wouldn't just break records—he would redefine the music industry forever.

A New Sound

After the massive success of Off the Wall in 1979, Michael knew his next record had to be bigger, better, and bolder. He didn't just want another hit—he wanted to make something revolutionary, something that no one had ever done before.

Michael teamed up once again with the legendary Quincy Jones, who had created Off the Wall. Together, they set out to create an album that would push limits, blending different styles of music like pop, rock, R&B, and funk into a sound that was fresh, exciting, and universal.

Michael was involved in every part of the process—from writing the words to perfecting the beats, from crafting the melodies to designing the album's visuals. He was determined to make a masterpiece. The result? Thriller, released on November 30, 1982.

From the time the album hit the shelves, it was clear that Thriller was something special. It had everything—catchy melodies, unforgettable rhythms, and powerful words. Michael took listeners on a journey with songs that ranged from romantic ballads to exciting dance tracks, from heart-pounding rock to eerie, cinematic storytelling.

Some of the best tracks included:
- "**Thriller**" – A spooky, cinematic song with a horror-movie theme and chilling narration by Vincent Price, a famous Hollywood actor known for his parts in scary films.
- "**Billie Jean**" – A mysterious, infectious song about a woman who claimed Michael was the father of her child, with an unforgettable bassline that became one of the most famous in music history.
- "**Beat It**" – A high-energy rock song featuring a legendary guitar solo by Eddie Van Halen, showing that Michael could blend rock and pop like no artist had before.
- "**Wanna Be Startin' Somethin'**" – A fast-paced, energetic track that mixed African beats with funk and pop, creating an electrifying sound.

- **"Human Nature"** – A soft, emotional ballad that showed Michael's incredible vocal range and sensitivity.
- **"P.Y.T**. (Pretty Young Thing)" – A fun, upbeat song with a funky groove that made fans want to dance.

With its groundbreaking mix of styles, innovative production, and unforgettable melodies, Thriller wasn't just an album—it was a global phenomenon.

Making History

As soon as Thriller was released, it started breaking records. But no one could have imagined just how big it would become.

Within a few months, Thriller shot to the top of the charts, sitting at No. 1 on the Billboard 200 for 37 weeks—a record that still stands today. It went on to become the best-selling record of all time, with over 70 million copies sold worldwide.Michael wasn't just selling records—he was changing the music business.

Breaking Racial Barriers

Before Thriller, MTV, the popular music television network, rarely played music videos by Black acts. But when Michael launched the videos for "Billie Jean", "Beat It", and later, "Thriller", everything changed.

MTV couldn't ignore Michael's brilliance—his music videos were more than just simple clips; they were mini-movies, filled with exciting plots, groundbreaking special effects, and unforgettable dance routines. His videos were so powerful

and innovative that MTV had no choice but to play them—
and in doing so, Michael helped open the door for future
Black acts on the channel.

The Groundbreaking Thriller Video

In December 1983, Michael released the music video for
"Thriller", and it became one of the most legendary
moments in showbiz history.

Directed by John Landis, a famous Hollywood director, the
"Thriller" video was unlike anything the world had ever seen
before. It was a 14-minute short film, containing a full
storyline, Hollywood-style special effects, and elaborate
dance sequences.

The video starts with Michael and his girlfriend walking
through the woods at night when he quickly transforms into
a werewolf. Later, in another shocking twist, he turns into a
zombie, leading a group of the undead in the most famous
dance performance of all time.

The zombie dance became an instant hit, and people all
over the world tried to learn the moves. To this day, the
"Thriller" dance is performed at Halloween parties, dance
contests, and flash mobs everywhere.

The impact of the Thriller video was massive—it proved that
music videos could be art, and it changed the way artists
treated visual storytelling forever.

A Night to Remember – The Grammy Awards
In 1984, Michael made history once again at the Grammy Awards, the most prestigious awards event in music.

Thriller won eight Grammy Awards—the most ever won by a single artist in one night. This included Album of the Year, Record of the Year, and Best Male Pop Vocal Performance.

Michael also won eight American Music Awards, three MTV Video Music Awards, and was even honored with a star on the Hollywood Walk of Fame.

By this time, Michael Jackson was no longer just a musician—he was a world icon.

The Moonwalk Magic
Even though Thriller was already making waves, one act would make Michael even more legendary.

On March 25, 1983, Michael appeared at the Motown 25: Yesterday, Today, Forever television special. It was a celebration of Motown Records, the label that had first found The Jackson 5.

Michael took the stage in his now-iconic outfit—a black sequined jacket, black pants, white socks, and a single white glove wrapped in crystals. As he sang "Billie Jean", the crowd was already mesmerized. But then, in one amazing moment, Michael did something that no one had ever seen before.

He glided backward easily across the stage—it was the Moonwalk.

The crowd went wild. People couldn't believe their eyes. How was he moving like that? Was it an illusion?

The Moonwalk became Michael's signature dance move, and it quickly made him a legend. Kids and adults everywhere tried to imitate it, and it became one of the most popular dance moves of all time.

That night, Michael earned his place in history. He wasn't just a singer or a dancer—he was an artist like no other.

Thriller wasn't just an album—it was a societal revolution. It broke records, shattered racial barriers, changed the way music videos were made, and gave the world some of the most iconic acts ever.

With its unforgettable songs, groundbreaking visuals, and Michael's unmatched ability, Thriller cemented his title as the King of Pop.

But Michael wasn't done yet. He would continue to grow, innovate, and inspire for years to come.

Chapter 5

The Power of Dance and Music

Michael Jackson wasn't just a singer—he was a performer like no other. His music, his dance moves, and his music videos weren't just entertainment; they were revolutionary. He made people feel, think, and dream. His songs carried powerful messages, and his dance moves seemed almost magical.

With every performance, Michael pushed the limits of what was possible in music and dance. He became more than just an artist—he became a global symbol of creativity, passion, and inspiration.

Signature Dance Moves
Michael Jackson's dancing was electrifying. He didn't just move—he told stories with his body. He could make even the smallest movements feel powerful and mesmerizing. From lightning-fast footwork to smooth, gliding motions, Michael created dance moves that became legendary.

The Moonwalk
One of Michael's most famous dance moves was the Moonwalk. When he performed it for the first time on television in 1983, the world was left in shock.

Michael appeared to be gliding backward effortlessly, as if he were defying gravity. His feet barely lifted off the ground, yet he moved as if he were floating on air. No one had ever seen anything like it.

Even though the Moonwalk had been used by other dancers before, Michael perfected it and made it his own. It became his signature move, and fans everywhere tried to copy it. To this day, it remains one of the most iconic dance moves in history.

The Toe Stand

Michael had incredible control over his body, and one move that proved it was the Toe Stand. He would smoothly lift himself onto the very tips of his toes, balancing effortlessly while striking a dramatic pose.

Most people can only stand on their toes for a second or two, but Michael could hold the position with perfect balance—making it look easy, even though it required extreme strength and skill.

The Anti-Gravity Lean

In his "Smooth Criminal" music video, Michael introduced another dance move that left people stunned—the Anti-Gravity Lean.

During the performance, he and his dancers leaned forward at a sharp angle, defying gravity itself. Audiences were left wondering: How did he do that?

Years later, it was revealed that Michael had invented a special shoe design that allowed him to perform the move. But even with special shoes, it required incredible core strength and precision to pull it off perfectly.

Other Iconic Moves
Michael had many other signature moves, including:

- **The Crotch Grab** – A bold, energetic move that became a signature part of his performances.
- The Side Glide – A variation of the Moonwalk, where he glided sideways instead of backward.
- **The Spin** – A rapid, tight spin that would often end with him stopping suddenly on his toes.
- **The Robot Dance** – Inspired by pop-locking and breakdancing, Michael made robotic movements look smooth and futuristic.

With his unmatched dance skills, Michael didn't just perform—he mesmerized. His moves became legendary, inspiring dancers and artists for generations to come.

Songs That Inspired the World
Michael's music was more than just catchy beats and melodies—it had a message. His songs spoke about love, unity, change, and hope. He wanted to make the world a better place, and his music reflected that.

Songs About Change and Unity
"Man in the Mirror" (1987) – One of Michael's most powerful songs, it encouraged people to look at themselves and make the world a better place. It became an anthem for self-reflection and change.

- *"Heal the World"* (1991) – This song was a heartfelt plea to help children and protect the planet. Michael even started a charity with the same name to help kids in need.
- *"Black or White"* (1991) – A song about racial equality, reminding the world that love has no color. The music video showed people of different races and cultures, celebrating diversity.

Songs That Gave People Strength
- *"Don't Stop 'Til You Get Enough"* (1979) – A song full of energy and excitement, encouraging people to enjoy life and keep going no matter what.
- *"Beat It"* (1982) – A song about avoiding violence and choosing a better path. It inspired young people to stay away from gangs and fights.
- *"They Don't Care About Us"* (1995) – A powerful song about injustice, speaking up for those who felt unheard.

Songs About Love and Emotion
- *"You Are Not Alone" (1995)* – A comforting song that reminded people that they are never truly alone.
- *"The Way You Make Me Feel" (1987)* – A fun, energetic song about the excitement of falling in love.
- *"Remember the Time" (1992)* – A beautiful song about cherishing special memories with someone you love.

Michael's music had the power to inspire, heal, and bring people together. His songs weren't just for entertainment—they had deep meaning that touched hearts around the world.

Music Videos Like No Other

Before Michael Jackson, music videos were simple performance clips. But Michael transformed music videos into cinematic masterpieces.

He didn't just make music videos—he made mini-movies with storytelling, special effects, and groundbreaking dance sequences.

"Thriller" (1983) – The Most Iconic Music Video Ever

The "Thriller" video was a game-changer. With its Hollywood-style production, zombies, and legendary dance routine, it became the most famous music video of all time.

It was 14 minutes long, making it the longest music video ever at the time. The combination of horror, humor, and dance made it an instant classic. Even today, people all over the world recreate the zombie dance every Halloween.

"Smooth Criminal" (1988) – The Anti-Gravity Lean

The "Smooth Criminal" video felt like a classic gangster movie, with Michael dressed in a white suit, surrounded by dancers in a 1930s nightclub.

It featured one of the most jaw-dropping moments in music video history—the Anti-Gravity Lean, where Michael and his dancers leaned forward at impossible angles.

"Black or White" (1991) – Pioneering Special Effects

The "Black or White" video was famous for its morphing technology, where people's faces smoothly transformed into different races and ethnicities. This had never been seen before in a music video and was a groundbreaking moment in digital effects.

"Bad" (1987) – A Powerful Street Dance Battle
Directed by Martin Scorsese, one of Hollywood's greatest filmmakers, "Bad" was a high-energy video featuring an intense street dance battle in a subway station. The choreography was raw, fast-paced, and full of attitude.

"Remember the Time" (1992) – An Egyptian Fantasy
This music video had a Hollywood cast, including actor Eddie Murphy and model Iman. Set in ancient Egypt, Michael performed stunning dance sequences in golden royal outfits, making it one of the most visually stunning music videos ever.

Chapter 6

Spreading Love and Helping Others

Michael Jackson wasn't just a musical genius—he was also a man with a big heart. Beyond his fame, his records, and his legendary performances, he was deeply committed to making the world a better place.

Michael believed that love and kindness were more important than anything else. He used his voice, not just to sing, but to speak up for those in need. Whether it was helping sick children, donating to charities, or raising awareness about global issues, Michael always found ways to give back.

He often said, "Heal the world, make it a better place," and he truly lived by those words.

Michael's Kind Heart
From a young age, Michael was taught the importance of caring for others. Even though he became a superstar at a young age, he never lost his sense of kindness and compassion.

His fame gave him a platform to reach millions of people, and he used it to spread messages of love, unity, and peace. He always treated his fans with kindness, taking the time to greet them, sign autographs, and listen to their stories.

Michael also had a special love for children. He believed that every child deserved to be happy, safe, and loved. He once said:

"Children show me in their playful smiles the divine in everyone. This simple goodness shines straight from their hearts."

Because of this, he dedicated much of his life to helping children who were sick, poor, or suffering in any way.

Neverland: A Place for Joy and Healing

One of the most beautiful examples of Michael's kindness was Neverland Ranch, his home in California.

Neverland wasn't just a place for Michael to live—it was a magical world created for children. Inspired by Peter Pan, the boy who never grew up, Michael wanted Neverland to be a place where kids could feel safe, happy, and free.

He built a zoo, an amusement park, and a movie theater so that children, especially those who were sick or underprivileged, could experience joy and wonder. He often invited groups of children to visit, giving them tours, gifts, and unforgettable memories.

For Michael, Neverland wasn't about luxury—it was about bringing smiles to children's faces.

Charity and Humanitarian Work

Michael didn't just talk about making the world a better place—he took action. He donated hundreds of millions of dollars to charities, supported hospitals, and helped people in need all over the world.

His generosity earned him a place in the Guinness World Records as the most charitable pop star in history. He supported over 39 charities throughout his life, including:

- *The Make-A-Wish Foundation* – Helped grant wishes to children with life-threatening illnesses.
- *USA for Africa* – Supported African communities struggling with poverty and famine.
- *The Elizabeth Taylor AIDS Foundation* – Raised awareness and funds for AIDS research.
- *The United Negro College Fund* – Helped provide education for African American students.

"We Are the World" – Singing for a Cause

In 1985, Michael co-wrote and performed "We Are the World", a song created to help starving people in Africa.

This was not just any song—it was a global movement. Michael gathered some of the biggest stars in music, including Lionel Richie, Stevie Wonder, and Diana Ross, to record the song together.

All the profits from the song went to charity, raising over $63 million to help fight hunger in Africa. It became one of the best-selling singles of all time and proved that music could truly change the world.

The lyrics were a powerful message of unity:
"We are the world, we are the children, we are the ones who make a brighter day, so let's start giving."

This song inspired millions of people to help those in need.

Helping Disaster Victims

Michael never ignored people who were suffering, especially after natural disasters.

- In 1988, he donated $600,000 to help people affected by an earthquake in Armenia.
- In 1992, after Hurricane Andrew struck Florida, he visited the affected communities and donated food, clothing, and supplies.
- In 2004, after the devastating Indian Ocean tsunami, Michael worked on a charity song called "From the Bottom of My Heart" to help survivors.

Whenever tragedy struck, Michael stepped up to help.

"Heal the World" – A Mission of Love
One of Michael's most famous and heartfelt songs was "Heal the World", released in 1991.

This song wasn't just music—it was a call for action. It urged people to care for one another, protect the planet, and help children in need.

Michael believed that the world could be a better place if everyone showed more love and kindness. He once said:

"I believe in us as a people. I know that we can make a difference in our world."

To turn his words into action, he created the Heal the World Foundation, a charity dedicated to:
- *Providing food, shelter, and medical care to children.*
- *Fighting poverty and hunger.*
- *Promoting peace and education.*

Michael's Famous Super Bowl Performance

In 1993, Michael performed at the Super Bowl halftime show, one of the biggest TV events in the world. Instead of just performing for entertainment, he used this moment to spread a message of love and unity.

During his performance, he sang "Heal the World" as a giant globe appeared on stage, symbolizing hope and peace. Hundreds of children from different backgrounds joined him, sending a message that the future was in their hands.This performance became one of the most memorable moments in Super Bowl history.

The Song's Lasting Impact

Even today, "Heal the World" is played at charity events, schools, and peace gatherings. It continues to inspire people to be kind and take care of each other.

Michael once said:
"If you want to make the world a better place, take a look at yourself and make a change."

His words still hold true today.

Chapter 7

The Neverland Dream

Michael Jackson was more than just a musician—he was a dreamer who believed in magic, innocence, and the joy of youth. As he grew older, he never wanted to lose that sense of wonder and fantasy. That dream came to life in Neverland Ranch, a house unlike any other.

Nestled in the beautiful countryside of Santa Barbara, California, Neverland Ranch was more than just a mansion —it was a magical world filled with excitement, fun, and the things that made Michael happiest. Inspired by the story of Peter Pan, Michael built a place where he and others could escape the pressures of the world and experience pure joy.

Neverland wasn't just for him—it was for children, families, and people in need. He wanted it to be a sanctuary, a place where kids who were sick or underprivileged could forget their problems and simply be kids.

A Home Like No Other

Michael purchased Neverland Ranch in 1988 and transformed it into a place that mirrored his love for fantasy, adventure, and childhood dreams. The ranch spanned nearly 3,000 acres of rolling hills, gardens, lakes, and forests. It wasn't just a house—it was a fantasy.

An Amusement Park in His Backyard

One of the most exciting things about Neverland was the entertainment park that Michael built inside his property. He filled it with:

- A Ferris wheel that lit up the night sky.
- A merry-go-round with beautifully made horses.
- A roller coaster that thrilled tourists.
- A train that took guests on a magical ride around the land.

Michael loved to bring joy to others, especially children who had never had the chance to visit a theme park. For them, Neverland was a dream come true.

A Private Movie Theater

Michael was a huge fan of movies and stories. He thought that movies could take people on magical journeys. So, he built a private movie theater inside Neverland, where he could watch films with his friends.

The theater wasn't just for his personal enjoyment—it was a place where sick and poor children could experience the magic of cinema. He often asked kids to special movie nights, where they could enjoy their favorite films with popcorn, candy, and a big comfy seat.

A Beautiful, Peaceful Place

Beyond the rides and fun, Neverland was a place of beauty and peace. It had:

- *A sparkling lake where swans floated across the water.*
- *Colorful flower fields that looked like they were from a fairy tale.*

- *A grand clock tower that played enchanting tunes.*
- *Secret paths and quiet spaces, where Michael could escape and think.*

For Michael, Neverland was not just a home—it was his haven, a place where he could be himself.

Loving Animals and Magic
Michael had a great love for animals. He believed they were gentle, loving, and amazing in their own way. At Neverland, he built his very own private zoo, where he cared for many exotic animals.

Michael's Animal Friends
Neverland's zoo was home to:
- **Bubbles the Chimp** – Michael's beloved pet chimpanzee, who was often seen by his side.
- **Louie the Llama** – A friendly llama that loved to roam the ranch.
- **Giraffes, tigers, and lions** – Rescued animals that Michael cared for.
- **Elephants, birds, and even a snake**!

Michael loved spending time with his animals, feeding them, playing with them, and treating them like family. He once said:

"Animals don't judge you. They don't hate. They just love you for who you are."

Many of the animals at Neverland were saved or given a second chance at life. Michael felt that all creatures deserved to be treated with kindness and respect.

Creating a World of Fantasy

Michael was fascinated by magic, fairy tales, and stories that transported people to different places. That's why Neverland was meant to feel like a storybook come to life.

The ranch was filled with statues of Peter Pan, ponds, and twinkling lights that made it feel truly magical. At night, the ranch glowed with lights, making it seem like a dreamland floating in the stars.

Michael once said:
"*My biggest inspiration comes from children. The magic, the wonder, and the mystery that they see in the world—that's what I try to bring to life.*"

Neverland was his way of keeping that magic alive, not just for himself but for everyone who visited.

Living Like Peter Pan

Michael often said that he connected to Peter Pan, the boy who never wanted to grow up.

Growing up in the spotlight, Michael never had a normal life. While other kids were playing, going to school, and having fun, Michael was rehearsing, singing, and traveling the world.

Because of this, he longed for the innocence of childhood, which is why he made Neverland. He wanted a place where he could finally experience the fun and freedom he had missed.

Bringing Happiness to Others

Michael didn't keep Neverland just for himself. He opened its doors to thousands of children, especially those who were sick, disabled, or from difficult situations.

He invited children from hospitals, orphanages, and charities to visit Neverland and feel the joy of:
- Riding the roller rides.
- Watching shows in the private theater.
- Playing games and visiting the beautiful gardens.

For many of these children, a visit to Neverland was a once-in-a-lifetime event. It gave them a chance to forget their pain and problems, even for just a little while.

Michael never wanted to grow up if it meant losing his sense of wonder. He thought that everyone should hold on to their inner child, no matter how old they were.

The Magic of Neverland Lives On

Even though Michael is no longer with us, the spirit of Neverland goes on.

It wasn't just a place—it was a sign of kindness, imagination, and giving. Michael's dream was to make the world a better, more magical place, and through Neverland, he did just that.

Michael's Legacy of Love and Joy

Michael believed that every person should feel joy, laughter, and wonder—not just children, but adults too. He showed the world that it's okay to believe in magic, to love animals, to play, and to dream.

Even today, his word continues to inspire millions:
- To spread kindness and love.
- To take care of animals and earth.
- To hold onto the magic of childhood.

Michael Jackson's Neverland Dream was not just about making a beautiful place—it was about creating a world where love, happiness, and imagination could shine forever.

As he once said:
"*The greatest thing you'll ever learn is just to love and be lo ved in return.*"

Chapter 8

Overcoming Challenges

Michael Jackson was one of the most beloved and successful musicians in history, but his journey was not always easy. Like anyone chasing their dreams, he faced difficult challenges along the way. From growing up in the public eye to dealing with criticism and personal struggles, Michael had to find strength, believe in himself, and keep going—no matter what.

Throughout his life, he proved that even in the hardest times, we can stay strong, rise above, and never give up.

Facing the Spotlight

Michael was only five years old when he started performing. While most kids were playing with toys, he was already singing, dancing, and rehearsing with his brothers in The Jackson 5. By the time he was a teenager, he was already one of the most famous people in the world.

Being famous may seem exciting, but it also comes with a lot of pressure. From a young age, Michael had to deal with:

- *Constant attention from the public and media.*
- *High expectations to always be perfect.*
- *Busy schedules with little time for a normal childhood.*

Even though he loved performing, there were times when he felt lonely. He often said that he missed out on the simple joys of childhood—going to school, making friends, and playing outside. But despite this, he never let these challenges stop him.

Instead of focusing on what he missed, Michael poured his heart into his music. He used his songs to express his emotions, tell stories, and connect with people all over the world.

Staying Strong

As Michael grew older, the pressures of fame only increased. People watched his every move, and the media often spread false stories and rumors about him. This could have made him feel discouraged, but he chose to focus on his passion for music and helping others.

Michael believed that staying strong meant:

- *Believing in yourself, even when others doubt you.*
- *Focusing on your dreams, no matter what challenges come your way.*
- *Surrounding yourself with people who love and support you.*

Finding Strength Through Music

Whenever Michael faced struggles, he turned to music. He believed that music had the power to heal, inspire, and bring people together. Some of his songs were written from his own experiences of overcoming hardships, such as:

"**Man in the Mirror**" – A song about self-reflection and making the world a better place.

"**You Are Not Alone**" – A comforting song that reminds people they are never truly alone.

"**Keep the Faith**" – A song about believing in yourself, even when things get tough.

Through his music, Michael inspired millions of people to stay strong and never give up.

Staying Positive Despite Criticism

Being in the spotlight meant that not everyone would always be kind. Sometimes, Michael faced harsh criticism from the media and people who didn't understand him. They judged the way he looked, the way he lived, and even his kindness.

But instead of fighting back with anger, Michael chose love and kindness. He once said:

"*People write negatives things because they feel that's what sells. Good news doesn't sell. But I don't worry about it. If I let it bother me, I'd be miserable.*"

He knew that no matter what people said, he had to stay true to himself.

Never Giving Up

Despite the obstacles he faced, Michael never gave up on his dreams. He continued to:

- Make groundbreaking music.
- Push the limits of dance and performance.
- Use his voice to inspire change.

Even when things were difficult, he never let fear or doubt stop him.

Overcoming Setbacks

There were times in Michael's career when things didn't go as planned. Sometimes, his health suffered due to stress and exhaustion. Other times, he had to take breaks from performing. But no matter what happened, he always came back stronger.

Even when the world seemed against him, he reminded himself—and others—to keep believing.

A Message of Hope

Michael wanted people to know that no matter how hard life gets, you should never give up on yourself or your dreams. His songs, speeches, and actions carried messages of hope, resilience, and love.

He once said:

"If you enter this world knowing you are loved and leave this world knowing the same, then everything that happens in between can be dealt with."

Michael's life was proof that even the biggest stars face struggles, but with strength, faith, and perseverance, anything is possible.

Michael's Legacy of Strength

Today, Michael Jackson's story continues to inspire people all over the world. He showed us that:

- Challenges are a part of life, but they don't have to stop us.
- Staying true to ourselves is more important than pleasing others.
- With passion, hard work, and love, we can overcome anything.

Michael's journey wasn't always easy, but he never stopped believing in himself and his purpose. He faced challenges with courage, grace, and a heart full of love—a lesson we can all learn from.

As he sang in one of his most powerful songs:

"Don't stop till you get enough."

Michael never stopped—and neither should we.

Chapter 9

The Legacy Lives On

Michael Jackson may no longer be with us, but his impact on music, dance, and the world will never fade. His songs continue to be played in homes, schools, concerts, and celebrations across the globe. His dance moves are still imitated by young performers. His message of love, kindness, and unity continues to inspire millions.

Even after his passing, Michael's legacy remains alive in the hearts of fans, musicians, and dancers who were influenced by his incredible talent and dedication. From the streets of small towns to the grand stages of major cities, his influence is everywhere.

Let's explore how Michael's music, spirit, and memory live on.

The Music That Never Fades
Michael Jackson's music is timeless. It doesn't matter if a song was recorded 30 years ago or just yesterday—his music still moves people of all ages. His songs continue to be streamed, played on the radio, and performed by artists around the world.

Some of the reasons why his music continues to thrive include:

- **Universal Messages** – Many of Michael's songs speak about love, hope, change, and self-belief, which are themes that never grow old.
- **Incredible Sound** – His unique voice, catchy melodies, and powerful lyrics make his music unforgettable.
- **Danceable Beats** – Michael's music makes people want to move. Whether it's "Billie Jean" or "Don't Stop 'Til You Get Enough," his beats are still as exciting as ever.
- **Generational Impact** – Parents who grew up listening to Michael now introduce his music to their children, passing it on to new generations.

Songs That Will Always Be Loved
Some of Michael's biggest hits remain iconic to this day:

- "*Thriller*" – The best-selling album of all time, with a title track that still plays every Halloween.
- "*Billie Jean*" – The song with the legendary moonwalk that changed the world of dance forever.
- "*Beat It*" – A song that blended rock and pop in a way no one had ever done before.
- "*Heal the World*" – A song that encourages kindness, unity, and making the world a better place.
- "Black or White" – A powerful song about racial equality and breaking barriers.

Michael's music continues to top charts, win awards, and influence new generations of artists.

Inspiring Generations

Michael wasn't just a musician—he was a visionary. He changed the way people saw entertainment, combining music, dance, and storytelling like never before.

Inspiring Future Artists

Many of today's biggest stars, such as Beyoncé, Usher, Bruno Mars, The Weeknd, and Justin Timberlake, credit Michael as one of their biggest influences. They studied his dance moves, stage performances, and vocal techniques, using them to shape their own careers.

Artists inspired by Michael often say:
- *"I wanted to be like Michael growing up."*
- *"His music taught me what it means to be a true performer."*
- *"Michael Jackson showed the world that music can change lives."*

A Role Model for Dancers

Michael's dance moves remain some of the most famous in history. He popularized moves like:
- **The Moonwalk** – A magical move that makes it look like he's gliding backward.
- **The Toe Stand** – Balancing on his tiptoes like a statue.
- **The Anti-Gravity Lean** – The impossible lean in "Smooth Criminal."

Even today, dancers continue to learn and master his techniques, and his choreography is performed on TV shows, competitions, and concerts.

Teaching Kindness and Unity

Michael's humanitarian work continues to inspire people of all ages. His songs and actions encourage kindness, equality, and giving back. Schools, charities, and organizations often use his music to spread messages of love and change.

His message was simple:
- *Love one another.*
- *Help those in need.*
- *Never stop believing in a better world.*

Because of his influence, many young people continue his mission, spreading love and kindness in their communities.

Remembering Michael

Michael Jackson may have left the world on June 25, 2009, but his spirit lives on forever. Fans, family, and fellow artists continue to celebrate his life and honor his contributions.

Annual Tributes and Celebrations

Every year, fans around the world gather to celebrate his birthday, his music, and his life. Some of the ways they honor him include:

- **Michael Jackson Tribute Concerts** – Artists perform his songs to keep his music alive.

Thriller Flash Mobs – Every Halloween, groups of people dress up and dance to "Thriller."

Charity Events in His Name – Fans continue his humanitarian work by donating to causes he cared about.

Michael Jackson's Influence in Pop Culture

Even today, Michael's influence can be seen everywhere:

- His costumes and dance moves are recreated in TV shows, commercials, and social media.
- His music is featured in movies, commercials, and video games.
- His Neverland Ranch remains a symbol of his creativity and imagination.
- His statues and murals stand in different parts of the world, showing how deeply he is loved.

The Message He Left Us

Michael wanted to leave behind more than just music—he wanted to change the world. He once said:

"My goal in life is to give to the world what I was lucky to receive: the ecstasy of divine union through my music and my dance."

He believed that music was a powerful tool that could bring people together, heal hearts, and inspire change.

His Message to Young Dreamers
Michael Jackson's story teaches us that:

- Dreams can come true if you work hard and believe in yourself.
- Music and art can make the world a better place.
- Even in difficult times, never stop spreading love and kindness.

A Legacy That Will Never Die
Michael Jackson's legacy is more than just hit songs and amazing dance moves. It's about changing lives, inspiring people, and spreading love.

His music will never fade. His message will never be forgotten. His influence will continue for generations to come.

As long as people continue to listen, dance, and be inspired by his story, Michael Jackson's spirit will always live on.

In His Own Words
"In a world filled with hate, we must still dare to hope.
In a world filled with anger, we must still dare to comfort.
In a world filled with despair, we must still dare to dream.
And in a world filled with distrust, we must still dare to believe."

Michael dared to believe—and because of him, the world will never be the same.

Chapter 10

Fun Extras!

This section is all about fun facts, music, and dance moves that make Michael Jackson an unforgettable legend! Get ready to dive into some cool trivia, jam out to his greatest hits, and even learn how to do his most famous dance move—the Moonwalk!

Fun Facts About Michael Jackson
Michael Jackson was one of the most fascinating and talented entertainers in history. Here are some fun and surprising facts about the King of Pop:

1. The Best-Selling Album of All Time
Michael's album Thriller (released in 1982) is the best-selling album in music history! It sold over 70 million copies worldwide and had some of his most famous songs, including Beat It, Billie Jean, and Thriller.

2. He Created Iconic Dance Moves
Michael didn't just perform—he changed the way people danced! He made moves like the Moonwalk, the Robot, and the Toe Stand legendary.

3. He Had a Pet Chimpanzee Named Bubbles

Michael loved animals and had a pet chimpanzee named Bubbles. Bubbles even traveled with Michael on tour and lived in his Neverland Ranch.

4. He Won Hundreds of Awards

Michael holds the Guinness World Record for being the most awarded music artist of all time. He won 13 Grammy Awards, 39 Guinness World Records, and over 400 other music awards!

5. He Was the First Black Artist to Have a Music Video on MTV

Before Michael, MTV mainly played rock music. But when his video for Billie Jean came out, it changed everything—it was the first music video by a Black artist to air regularly on MTV.

6. He Had a Voice That Broke Records

Michael could sing in four different vocal ranges! His voice was so unique that no one could copy his exact sound.

7. He Wrote "We Are the World" to Help People in Need

Michael co-wrote We Are the World, a charity song that raised millions of dollars for people struggling with hunger in Africa. The song featured many famous singers and became a worldwide anthem for helping others.

8. He Had His Own Theme Park at Neverland Ranch

Michael's home, Neverland Ranch, was like a real-life fairy tale! It had an amusement park, a zoo, and even a movie theater where he invited children to come and have fun.

9. He Performed for Over 500,000 People in a Single Concert

During his 1988 Bad World Tour, Michael performed in Germany for over 500,000 fans—one of the biggest concert audiences ever!

10. He Loved Cartoons and Superheroes

Even as an adult, Michael loved watching cartoons like Tom and Jerry and was a big fan of Spider-Man!

Michael's Greatest Hits Playlist

Michael Jackson's music is timeless, and his songs are still loved by people of all ages! Here's a playlist of his greatest hits that will get you dancing and singing along:

1. Thriller (1982)

The ultimate Halloween song and the best-selling single of all time!

2. Billie Jean (1982)

One of Michael's biggest hits, featuring his smooth dance moves and the first-ever Moonwalk performance!

3. Beat It (1982)

A song with an amazing guitar solo that inspired people to stand up for themselves.

4. Smooth Criminal (1987)

Famous for its gravity-defying lean in the music video!

5. Bad (1987)
Michael's song about proving yourself and standing strong.

6. Black or White (1991)
A song about unity and equality, with a music video that amazed the world!

7. Man in the Mirror (1987)
A powerful song about changing the world by changing yourself first.

8. Don't Stop 'Til You Get Enough (1979)
One of his earliest solo hits, full of energy and fun!

9. Heal the World (1991)
A song that encourages everyone to spread kindness and help those in need.

10. Rock with You (1979)
A smooth and soulful song that makes you want to dance all night!

Put on your headphones, turn up the volume, and feel the magic of Michael Jackson's music!

Learn How to Moonwalk!
One of the most famous dance moves in history is the Moonwalk, and Michael Jackson made it legendary! Want to learn how to do it? Follow these simple steps:

Step 1: Start in Position
- Stand up straight with your feet close together.
- Keep your back foot (right foot) on its toes and your front foot (left foot) flat on the floor.

Step 2: The Slide
- Push down with your back foot's toes and slide your front foot (left) backward smoothly.
- Keep your front foot flat and let your back foot stay on its toes.

Step 3: Switch Feet
- Once your front foot moves back, switch positions:
- Put your right foot flat on the ground.
- Lift your left foot on its toes (so now your left foot is the back foot).

Step 4: Repeat and Keep It Smooth
- Keep switching feet and sliding backward smoothly— like you're gliding on ice!
- Make sure your upper body stays still and relaxed while your legs do all the work.

Step 5: Add Style!
- Tilt your head, snap your fingers, or add a spin at the end—just like Michael did!
- Practice in front of a mirror to make it even smoother.

Pro Tip: It takes practice, so don't give up! Michael practiced for hours before performing the Moonwalk for the first time. Keep trying, and soon you'll be Moonwalking like a pro!

SELF REFLECTIVE PROMPTS

1. Michael Jackson started performing at a young age. What is a talent or skill you have that you would love to develop?

_____

_____

_____

_____

_____

2. Michael faced challenges and criticism but never gave up. Can you think of a time when something was difficult for you? How did you push through?

_____

_____

_____

_____

_____

_____

3. Sometimes people doubt us, just like they doubted Michael. How do you stay confident in yourself even when others don't believe in you?

_____

_____

_____

_____

_____

_____

4. Michael worked hard despite facing challenges. How do you handle failure or setbacks?

_____

_____

_____

_____

_____

_____

5. Michael expressed himself through music and dance. How do you like to express yourself (e.g., art, writing, sports, dance, music)?

_____

_____

_____

_____

_____

_____

6. Michael used music to tell stories and share emotions. If you could write a song or a story, what would it be about?

_____

_____

_____

_____

_____

_____

7. Michael believed in making the world a better place. What's one thing you can do today to help someone else?

_____

_____

_____

_____

_____

_____

8. Michael's song Heal the World talks about making a difference. How can small acts of kindness make the world a better place?

_____

_____

_____

_____

_____

_____

9. Michael performed in front of huge crowds. What's something that makes you nervous, and how can you build your confidence to face it?

_____

_____

_____

_____

_____

_____

10. If you could give yourself one piece of advice about believing in yourself, what would it be?

_____

_____

_____

_____

_____

_____

11. If you could create your own dance move like the Moonwalk, what would it be called, and how would it look?

_____

_____

_____

_____

_____

_____

12. Music helped Michael connect with people. How does music make you feel, and how do you use it in your daily life?

_____

_____

_____

_____

_____

_____

_____

13. What kind of impact do you want to have on the world when you grow up?

_____

_____

_____

_____

_____

_____

14. Imagine someone writing a book about your life one day. What do you hope they say about you?

_____

_____

_____

_____

_____

_____

_____

15. What is the biggest lesson you've learned from Michael Jackson's story, and how can you apply it to your own life?

_____

_____

_____

_____

_____

_____

16. If you could talk to Michael Jackson and ask him one question, what would it be, and why?

_____

_____

_____

_____

_____

_____

Printed in Great Britain
by Amazon

60586351R00047